THE TOUGHEST GMAT PRACTICE TEST
WE'VE EVER SEEN
VOLUME I

Dr. Nancy L. Nolan

* The GMAT is a registered trademark of the Graduate Management Admission Council (GMAC), which was not involved in the production of, and does not endorse, this publication.

Copyright 2011.

All rights reserved. No part of this book may be reproduced or transmitted in any form or by any means, electronic or mechanical, including photocopying, recording or by any information storage and retrieval system without written permission from the author except for the inclusion of brief quotations in a review.

Paperback, electronic and CD-ROM versions published by:

Magnificent Milestones, Inc.
www.ivyleagueadmission.com

ISBN: 9781933819617

Disclaimers:

(1) This book was written as a guide; it does not claim to be the definitive word on GMAT™ preparation. The opinions expressed are the personal observations of the author based on her own experiences. They are not intended to prejudice any party. Accordingly, the author and publisher do not accept any liability or responsibility for any loss or damage that have been caused, or allegedly caused, through the use of information in this book.

(2) The GMAT is a registered trademark of the Graduate Management Admission Council (GMAC), which sponsors the test and decides how it will be constructed, administered and used. Neither Dr. Nolan nor Magnificent Milestones, Inc. is affiliated with the GMAC.

(3) Admission to business school depends on several factors in addition to a candidate's GMAT™ scores (including GPA, recommendations, interview and essays). The author and publisher cannot guarantee that any applicant will be admitted to any specific school or program if (s)he follows the information in this book.

Dedication

For students everywhere;
may the size of your dreams be exceeded only
by your tenacity to attain them.

Acknowledgements

I am deeply indebted to the students, professors, counselors and admissions officers who have shared their perceptions and frustrations about the GMAT™. This book, which was written on your behalf, would not be nearly as powerful without your generous and insightful input.

I also want to thank my colleagues at www.ivyleagueadmission.com for providing a constant source of support, along with the best editorial help in the business.

Chapter 1: Introduction to the GMAT™

The GMAT is a 3- hour and 30- minute exam that is designed to test your reading, writing and mathematical skills. The exam is divided into three sections - Verbal, Quantitative and Analytical Writing. Except for the writing section, which requires students to write two original essays, the questions are primarily in multiple-choice format (students must select the correct answer from five possibilities).

The **Verbal Section** of the GMAT includes 41 multiple choice questions, which are presented in one 75-minute segment. They will include:

12 Reading Comprehension questions
13 Critical Reasoning questions
16 Sentence Correction questions

The **Quantitative Section** of the GMAT includes 37 questions, which are presented in one 75-minute section. They will include:

22 Mathematical Word Problems
15 Data Sufficiency questions

The **Analytical Writing Section** of the GMAT includes 2 essay prompts, which require students to write two original essays within 60-minutes. They will include an:

Analysis of an Issue
Analysis of an Argument

Throughout the Verbal and Quantitative sections of the exam, the GMAT will also include experimental questions, which the writers are "testing" for future editions of the exam. These questions will not count toward your score. Unfortunately, you will not know which questions on the GMAT are experimental when you take the exam, because they will look the same as the other questions. Consequently, you should never try to guess which questions are experimental; instead, you should tackle *every* question with the expectation that it will count.

For the Verbal and Quantitative sections of the GMAT, you will earn individual scores between 200 and 800. For the Analytical Writing Section, you will receive a score between 0 and 6.

Preparing for the Test

To achieve a top score of the GMAT, students should follow a three-step plan:

- Learn the concepts that are on the test
- Learn the tips, traps and strategies of the test writers
- Learn to work faster and smarter by taking timed practice tests

We address Steps 1 and 2 in our companion publication, *Guerrilla Tactics for the GMAT: Secrets and Strategies the Test Writers Don't Want You to Know.* From our experience, no one should take the GMAT without mastering these techniques, which can make the difference between a great score and a mediocre one.

To build your confidence and increase your speed with difficult question types (Step 3), we recommend *Guerrilla Review for the GMAT: 1,001 Practice Questions & Answers,* which presents the material under actual testing conditions. From our experience, working with sample questions isn't enough; you need to attack the questions *exactly* as they are presented on the GMAT. By design, we have organized the 1,001 GMAT questions in the identical format you will see on the exam:

For students who need additional practice for the quantitative section of the exam, *Math Word Problems for the GMAT: When Plugging Numbers into Formulas Just Isn't Enough* offers a complete review of the thirty types of word problems you are likely to see, including 600 sample problems. Through this publication, you will learn how to answer these questions quickly and accurately on the day of the test.

Finally, for students who are comfortable with the concepts on the GMAT and **really** want to challenge themselves before the big day, we are delighted to offer **this** publication, *The Toughest GMAT Practice Test We've Ever Seen*. Use this publication – and complete the mock exam - AFTER you have completed your preparation program. See how your performance compares to that of other highly competitive students.

What Makes a Question "Tough?"

If you've read our companion publications, you know that the GMAT tests the same concepts over and over again – and presents the same tricks, traps, and pitfalls on every exam. The questions on this "tough test" are the worst of the bunch because they are confusing, tedious, time-consuming......and difficult to assess. For the average student, they are the ones that you either "skip" in the interest of time or simply "guess" because you don't know how to approach them (or you got stuck somewhere in the verbiage). They are the annoying questions that keep you up at night because you know in your heart that you *should* have gotten them right.

Relax. That's what this exam is for – to show you the worst that the GMAT will throw at you, with a complete explanation and plan of attack for every problem. Our best recommendation is to tackle this exam AFTER you have read our other publications, reviewed all of the concepts on the test, and completed hundreds of sample problems. Otherwise, there's a good chance these questions will overwhelm you and possibly breed discouragement, which is definitely *not* our goal.

Instead, we want you to tackle this exam from a position of strength (rather than weakness), which you can only do if you are fully prepared for the battle. Take the time to review the concepts on the GMAT and to learn the typical tricks, traps and pitfalls that the test writers are most likely to use. Then, use this material for all it is worth – a chance to earn a top score and gain admission to the most prestigious business schools in the nation.

Chapter 2: The Practice Test

From our experience, the best way to build your confidence and speed before the GMAT is to take this mock exam *under actual testing conditions*. Go to a quiet place where you can work without interruption. Set a timer to the exact limit for each section - and adhere to it. Finally, limit yourself to the same resources you will be allowed to use at the test center. Your goal is to duplicate the actual testing conditions that you will encounter at the actual GMAT.

At the end of each section, we present a comprehensive answer key (including explanations) for every question. Use this mock exam to:

a. analyze your strengths
b. overcome your deficiencies
c. master the tricks and traps of each section of the exam
d. get the score you deserve

Good luck!

Verbal Section: 75 minutes 41 questions

Directions: The passages below are followed by questions based on their content. Answer the questions, based on what is *stated* or *implied* in the passage and any introductory material that may be provided.

Passage 1

Voegtlin some time ago tried to demonstrate that Vitamin B was identical with secretin and stimulated pancreatic flow, yet recent work at the Johns Hopkins University by Cowgill and by Aurep and Drummond in England has failed to confirm this. One of its most marked immediate effects is increase in appetite. Proux in Mendel's laboratory has shown that dogs which refused their basal diet would resume eating it if they were allowed to ingest separately a little dried yeast. Proux studied the metabolism of these dogs as regards nitrogen partition but the results give little data that is explicatory of the behavior of the vitamin. In 1915, Truitt was able to bring about marked immediate improvement and the ultimate recovery of a number of infants who were of the marasmic type by merely increasing the "B" vitamin content of their food.

10

In these cases, the vitamin was carried by Lloyd's reagent and administered mixed with cereal, or the crude extract was combined with the milk. The pancreas of the sheep was the source used. In these cases the growth curve changed abruptly from a decline to a sharp rise and this increase in weight continued and was accompanied by all the other signs of improved nutrition including increase in appetite. The change in the growth curve from decline to rise was accomplished without increasing or changing the basal diet but as the appetite increased the food had naturally to be increased to keep pace. In these cases, the effect of the vitamin was to enable the child to utilize its normal food and to increase its appetite for it. This action certainly suggests stimulation of the digestive glands. It also showed that even though the diet may contain the vitamin as was the case in the milk fed to these children the addition of the vitamin in concentrated form often gives an upward push that the food mixture fails to accomplish.

22

Daniels and Byfield have recently confirmed the effect of increased "B" in infant growth. Cramer has suggested in a paper published recently in the *American Journal of Physiology* that the fatty tissue about the suprarenals may be a depository of vitamin and that in the absence of vitamin this tissue loses its supply and that this is the explanation of lessened activity of that gland in certain metabolic disturbances. This idea tends to support the idea that vitamins are gland stimulants or hormones and the term "food hormone" has been suggested to describe them on that account. A few years ago Calkins and Eddy tried to determine the effect of the vitamin on the single cell by use of the paramecium but the results of the experiments failed to show a vitamin requirement on the part of these animals.

32

McDougall has recently suggested that the vitamins produce their effect on yeast cells by increasing hydration. Unfortunately, nearly all stimuli which produce growth are accompanied by hydration effects, thus, it is difficult to feel that this is a specific vitamin effect without denying the possibility. McDermott has tried to show that vitamins have a relation to oxidation effects. He observed that polyneuritic birds showed a marked reduction in catalase which was restorable by curing the birds with vitamin B. The main difficulty lies in the confluxibility of factors that function between cause and effect.

40

These views are at best speculations. The literature is singularly lacking in detailed metabolic analyses of excreta of animals during vitamin stimulation and we know nothing of the possibilities of overdose, for in all the work done, it has been generally assumed that the presence of an amount greater than that necessary to produce normal growth is not material. The exact manner of the vitamin's actions then remains to be determined.

46

1. Which of the following best expresses the author's opinion on Vitamin B's functionality?

    a. It has been definitively shown to catalyze appetite, human growth, and hydration in controlled studies.
    b. It has been linked to hydration in yeast cells in human infants and polyneuritic birds.
    c. It has been linked to appetite stimulation, human growth, and hydration in laboratory studies, but its precise role in these functions has yet to be determined.
    d. Depending on the dosage and substrate, it stimulates growth in human infants.
    e. Through hydration, it plays an intriguing role in appetitive stimulation and human growth.

2. According to the author, what did scientists at Johns Hopkins conclude about vitamin B?

    a. It stimulated the suprarenal glands.
    b. It did not stimulate pancreatic flow.
    c. It increased the appetite of dogs.
    d. It was identical to secretin.
    e. It did not increase the appetite of dogs.

3. What conclusion did the author draw from Truitt's work?

    a. Vitamin B stimulated the digestive glands of the subjects.
    b. He yielded little data that explained the behavior of Vitamin B in humans.
    c. Vitamin B serves as a nitrogen partition in canine digestion.
    d. Fatty tissue in infants is a depository of Vitamin B.
    e. Vitamin B is essential to the growth of single-celled organisms.

4. Which scientist linked a deficiency of Vitamin B to metabolic disturbances?

    a. Calkins
    b. Cowgill
    c. Cramer
    d. Mendel
    e. Voegtlin

5. Which information, if true, would dispute McDougall's conclusions?

    a. Vitamin B is an anti-oxidant.
    b. The effect was most pronounced in subjects with large amounts of fatty tissue.
    c. Hydration is not a vitamin-specific effect.
    d. There are numerous types and sources of Vitamin B, including dried yeast.
    e. The effect was only observed when subjects ingested the vitamin in concentrated form.

6. On Line 38, what does *confluxibility* mean?

    a. Confirmation
    b. Connectedness
    c. Disparity
    d. Irony
    e. Regression

7. Which of the following studies was NOT mentioned in the passage?

    a. The effect of vitamin B on infant growth
    b. The effect of vitamin B on catalase production
    c. The effect of vitamin B on a single cell
    d. The effect of different doses of vitamin B
    e. The nutritional impact of vitamin B from different sources

Passage 2

The eleventh century, during which feudal power rose to its height, was also the period when a reaction set in among the townspeople against the nobility. The spirit of Rome revived with that of the bourgeois and infused a feeling of opposition to the system which followed the conquest of the Teutons. "But," says M. Henri Martin, "what reappeared was not the Roman municipality of the Empire, stained by servitude, although surrounded with glittering pomp and gorgeous arts, but it was something coarse and almost semi-barbarous in form, though strong and generous at its core, and which, as far as the difference of the times would allow, rather reminds us of the small republics which existed previous to the Roman Empire."

Two strong impulses, originating from two totally dissimilar centers of action, irresistibly propelled this great social revolution, with its various and endless aspects, affecting all of central Europe, and being more or less felt in the west, the north, and the south. On one side, the Greek and Latin partiality for ancient corporations, modified by a democratic element, and an innate feeling of opposition characteristic of barbaric tribes; and on the other, the free spirit and equality of the old Celtic tribes rising suddenly against the military hierarchy, which was the offspring of conquest. Europe was roused by the double current of ideas which simultaneously urged her on to a new state of civilization, and more particularly, to a new organization of city life.

Italy was naturally destined to be the country where the new trials of social regeneration were to be made, but she presented the greatest variety of customs, laws, and governments, including the Emperor, Pope, bishops, and feudal princes. In Tuscany and Liguria, the march towards liberty was continued almost without effort; whilst in Lombardy, on the contrary, the feudal resistance was most powerful. Everywhere, however, cities became more or less completely enfranchised, though some more rapidly than others. In Sicily, feudalism swayed over the countries, but in the greater part of the peninsula, the democratic spirit of the cities influenced the enfranchisement of the rural population. The feudal caste was in fact dissolved; the barons were transformed into patricians of the noble towns which gave their republican magistrates the old title of consuls.

The Teutonic Emperor in vain sought to seize and turn to his own interest the sovereignty of the people, who had shaken off the yokes of his vassals: the signal of war was immediately given by the newly enfranchised masses and the imperial eagle was obliged to fly before the banners of the besieged cities. Happy indeed might the cities of Italy have been had they not forgotten, in their prosperity, that union alone could give them the possibility of maintaining that liberty which they so freely risked in continual quarrels amongst one another.

8. What is the main point of the passage?

    a. Despite the opposition, Italians refused to relinquish their freedom
    b. The Italian social revolution was guided by two strong, but mutually opposing, forces
    c. Without unity, the Italian cities were unable to maintain their liberty
    d. The eleventh century was a period of great wealth and refinement in Italy
    e. The democratic spirit in Italian cities eventually conquered the feudalistic tendencies in rural areas

9. According to M. Henri Martin, the entity that appeared in Italy after the fall of the Roman Empire was characterized by all of the following EXCEPT:

    a. Coarseness
    b. Generosity
    c. Semi-barbaric
    d. Stained by servitude
    e. Strength

10. According to the author, which two impulses propelled the European social revolution?

    a. Celtic conquests versus Greek and Latin democracy
    b. Celtic barbarism versus Greek and Latin corporations
    c. Celtic military versus Greek and Latin barbarism
    d. Celtic conquest of Greek and Latin democracy
    e. Celtic spirit of freedom and equality versus Greek and Latin opposition

11. According to the author, Italian society in the eleventh century included all of the following EXCEPT:

    a. Feudal princes
    b. Sicilian priests
    c. Bishops
    d. Emperor
    e. Pope

12. In Line 30, to what does the word "*yokes*" refer?

    a. Garments
    b. Ideology
    c. Weapons
    d. Values
    e. Oppression

Directions: The questions in this section are based on the reasoning contained in brief statements or passages. For some questions, more than one of the choices could conceivably answer the question. However, you are to choose the one that provides the most complete and accurate answer. You should not make assumptions that are implausible, superfluous, or incompatible with the passage.

13. For many years, historians insisted that Asian women in the 1700s adhered to a rigid vegetarian diet, including roots, nuts, and berries. However, a recent study of their remains suggests that this might not be true. Hair samples from an Asian female revealed significant levels of Vitamins D and K, which the human body cannot product on its own; further, the only dietary source of these vitamins is red meat. Therefore, it is likely that Asian women from the 1700s consumed a meat-based diet, rather than vegetarian fare.

Which of the following, if true, would strengthen this conclusion the most?

    a. A recent nutritional study suggests that the human body can manufacture minute amounts of Vitamin D in frigid climates.
    b. The levels of Vitamin D and K in the hair samples from the Asian female were identical to those from women in Europe who eat a meat-based diet.
    c. When scientists re-ran the analyses on the same samples, they obtained identical results.
    d. When scientists examined hair samples from the bodies of several other Asian women, they obtained identical results.
    e. Twelve years after scientists examined the hair samples and published their results, no one has disputed them.

14. An author who was writing a book about left-handedness solicited participants for a survey in *USA Today*. One-hundred left-handed readers agreed to be interviewed and assessed for certain personality traits. As the writer suspected, the interview results and personality assessments showed that Southpaws were more emotional and accident-prone than random samples of the general population. These findings support the conclusion that people are affected by their natural handedness.

Which one of the following selections, if true, points out the most critical weakness in the method used by the author to investigate left-handed characteristics?

   a. Left-handed children are typically more emotional than their right-handed siblings.
   b. The interviews and assessments were performed by an outside firm, not by the author himself.
   c. People who saw the newspaper ad were more likely to be left-handed than the number of Southpaws in the general population.
   d. The author's bias against left-handed people reinforced his initial impression of their character traits.
   e. Readers who were not emotional and accident-prone were less likely to respond to the author's newspaper ad or participate in the study.

15. The number of uninsured Americans has dramatically increased in recent years. In 2001, 20 million Americans had no medical insurance. In 2006, however, 50 million Americans had no insurance. These statistics prove that 30 million Americans lost their medical insurance between 2001 and 2006.

Which one of the following does the author assume in reaching his conclusion?

   a. The rising number of uninsured Americans will create an unprecedented economic crisis.
   b. Due to financial constraints, fewer employers offer medical insurance as an employee benefit.
   c. The increase in the number of uninsured Americans was not due to the increase in population.
   d. Between 2001 and 2005, hospitals reported a similar increase in the number of uninsured patients.
   e. For several years prior to 2001, most Americans received health coverage from their employers.

16. All cooks eat shrimp. Joy is a cook. Therefore, Joy must eat shrimp.

Which of the following statements uses a similar type of reasoning?

   a. All laws are regulations. Rules are also regulations. Therefore, rules must be laws.
   b. All begonias are flowers. Some begonias are yellow. Therefore, this begonia is a flower.
   c. All models are tall. Patricia is a model. Therefore, Patricia must be tall.
   d. All coins are nickel. Nickel is a natural metal. Therefore, all coins are natural metal.
   e. All students are smart. Julia is smart. Therefore, Julia must be a student.

17. Patients with lung cancer who consume citrus fruits such as oranges and pears often suffer from dire complications during chemotherapy, such as nausea and dizziness. Over time, they are unable to tolerate such high doses of these cancer fighting drugs. In contrast, patients with pancreatic cancer who consume a comparable amount of citrus fruits such as oranges and pears do not suffer from similar complications during chemotherapy.

Which one of the following, if true, does the most to resolve the apparent discrepancy in the argument above?

   a. Patients with pancreatic cancer are deficient in Vitamins A and C, which citrus fruit provides.
   b. Most chemotherapy drugs contain iron, which makes the vitamins in citrus fruit impossible to absorb.
   c. Patients with lung cancer have an enzymatic abnormality that causes nausea and dizziness when they consume citrus fruit.
   d. Females are far more likely than males to contract lung cancer.
   e. The reaction is far less likely to occur if chemotherapy is administered in the earliest stages of tumor growth.

18. Some students are athletes. All athletes are limber. Therefore, this student must be limber.

Which of the following uses a similar type of flawed reasoning?

   a. All houses have walls. Some houses are large. Therefore, large houses must have walls.
   b. Some flyers are travelers. All travelers are old. Therefore, this flyer must be old.
   c. Some months have thirty days. All months have four weeks, Therefore, last month had thirty days.
   d. Some fruits are fattening. An orange is a fruit. Therefore, an orange must be fattening.
   e. All plants are green. Some weeds are orange. Therefore, this plant must be a weed.

19. Sophia cannot write the article because she has already accepted another freelance assignment. Francesca, on the other hand, cannot write the article because she is not fluent in Italian. So, the article must be assigned to Miranda, who is the only *Newsweek* editor in the Tokyo office, other than Sophia and Francesca.

The argument depends on which of the following assumptions?

   a. The editors in the Tokyo office do not need to speak Italian.
   b. *Newsweek* editors are permitted to accept freelance assignments.
   c. The article must be written by a *Newsweek* editor in the Tokyo office.
   d. Miranda does not accept freelance assignments.
   e. Sophia, Miranda and Francesca are all freelance journalists.

20. Everything that is multifaceted and majestic fails to impress her, so there are things that fail to impress her that are magenta.

The conclusion of the argument follows logically if which one of the following is assumed?

   a. Some majestic things are magenta, but not multifaceted.
   b. Some things that are multifaceted and majestic are magenta.
   c. Some multifaceted things are magenta, but not majestic.
   d. All magenta things fail to impress her.
   e. Everything multifaceted is magenta.

21. Attorney: To determine the validity of his client's personal injury claim, my opponent wants to review 300 other cases in which the complainant suffered a similar type of injury. He will personally contact all 300 victims to verify whether or not they were permanently paralyzed from using my client's product over the past ten years. But this type of after-the-fact inquiry is unfair and capricious because it does not consider the numerous other factors that influence the respondents' health, including age, lifestyle, and pre-existing conditions. Therefore, I submit that that the results of the attorney's review should not be accepted into evidence because they will unfairly prejudice the jury.

Which of the following, if true, would most help to justify the attorney's argument?

   a. Many of the previous complainants settled their cases out of court because the evidence in their cases was slim.
   b. The admission of hearsay evidence is precluded by state law.
   c. Several previous juries were swayed by the results of identical reviews.
   d. The defendant in the case waived his right to a jury trial on similar charges in the past.
   e. It is impossible to determine cause and effect ten years after an injury.

22. According to epidemiologists, the United States population is struck by a global pandemic, such as typhoid fever or swine flu, on an average of once every fifty years. The last such incident occurred in 2009, when swine flu claimed the lives of several Americans who lived along the Texas-Mexico border. Thus, we can reasonably expect that the United States population will not be struck by another pandemic until 2059, when public health experts will be better prepared to predict and treat the type of patients who are affected by the illness. Hence, it would be foolish to allocate immediate funds to swine flu research in the near future, when we face more pressing needs, such as the rapid proliferation of HIV/AIDS.

The reasoning in the argument is most subject to criticism on what grounds?

   a. It implies that some diseases are more important than others.
   b. It does not consider the theoretical value of epidemiological research, only the preventive value.
   c. It does not consider the health status of people outside the United States.
   d. It fails to provide valid statistical data to support its claims.
   e. It uses evidence about the average frequency of a pandemic to make a specific prediction about when the next pandemic will occur.

23. In 2005, a large state university raised its tuition and fees by 5% for most undergraduate students. The following year, school administrators imposed an additional 5% tuition hike for the same students. Despite these consecutive tuition hikes, the total amount of money collected by the university in tuition and fees remained constant until 2007, when it decreased dramatically.

Each of the following, if true, could help to resolve the apparent discrepancy described above EXCEPT:

   a. Beginning in 2007, the tuition and fees for scholarship students were deposited into a different account, which artificially deflated the number that was reported in the study.
   b. The increase in tuition and fees caused a drop in enrollment in 2007.
   c. The tuition increases were waived for all students who pre-enrolled for classes.
   d. The total enrollment at the university increased dramatically in 2007.
   e. In 2007, the university eliminated several undergraduate programs, which had formerly attracted hundreds of students.

24. Twelve thousand patients with seafood allergies were evaluated for a variety of viral infections. The physicians who examined them discovered that 90% of the patients with seafood allergies also tested positive for the Epstein Barr virus. These findings support the conclusion that seafood allergies cause the Epstein Barr virus.

Which one of the following selections, if true, points out the most critical weakness in the method used by the physician?

   a. He confused correlation with causation.
   b. He generalized from a very small sample to a large population.
   c. He used circular reasoning.
   d. He did not publish his study in a peer-reviewed journal.
   e. He intentionally chose a biased population for his study.

25. Most exterminators who are experienced beekeepers are ambidextrous, but some non-ambidextrous exterminators are also experienced beekeepers. In addition, every experienced beekeeper is a licensed taxidermist.

If the statements in the argument are true, which of the following must also be true?

   a. Some licensed taxidermists are ambidextrous.
   b. Every licensed taxidermist is ambidextrous.
   c. Most exterminators are licensed taxidermists.
   d. Every licensed taxidermist is an exterminator.
   e. The experienced beekeepers who are licensed taxidermists are also ambidextrous.

26. The Hampton Inn has no vacant rooms because they are hosting the history convention. The Hilton, on the other hand, has no vacancies because they are hosting the tri-state job fair. So, the visitors from the technical conference will have to stay at the Sheraton, which is the only five-star hotel in San Francisco besides the Hampton Inn and the Hilton.

The argument depends on which of the following assumptions?

   a. If the history convention was cancelled, the Hampton Inn could accommodate the visitors from the technical conference.
   b. There is a shortage of hotel rooms for business travelers in San Francisco.
   c. The Hilton and Hampton Inn offer attractive discounts to corporate travelers.
   d. The visitors from the technical conference can only stay at a five-star hotel in San Francisco.
   e. The Sheraton in San Francisco is less popular than the Hampton Inn and Hilton.

Directions: The following sentences test correctness and effectiveness of expression. Part of each sentence (or the entire sentence) is underlined; beneath each sentence are five ways of phrasing the underlined material. Choice A repeats the original phrasing; the other four choices are different. If you think the original phrasing produces a better sentence than the alternatives, select choice A; if not, select one of the other choices. In making your selection, follow the requirements of standard written English, such as grammar, choice of words, sentence construction, and punctuation. Your selection should result in the most effective sentence – clear and precise, without awkwardness or ambiguity.

Example: Most teenagers struggle to be free both of parental domination but also from premature responsibilities.

   a. both of parental domination but also from premature responsibilities.
   b. both of parental domination and also from premature responsibilities.
   c. both of parental domination and also of premature responsibilities.
   d. of parental domination and premature responsibilities.
   e. both of parental domination and their premature responsibilities as well.

The correct answer is Choice D.

27. Even before the Rockettes rehearsed their dance performance, they knew that they were not prepared for such an important performance.

   a. they knew that they were not prepared
   b. they knew that they did not prepare
   c. they knew that they had not been prepared
   d. they knew that they had not prepared
   e. they had known that they were not prepared

28. That which we cannot do without is that which binds us.

   a. That which we cannot do without is that which binds us.
   b. That we cannot do without binds us to it.
   c. Which we cannot do without binds us to it.
   d. What we cannot do without is that which binds us.
   e. We are bound by what we cannot do without.

29. Either Stephanie or him is waiting.

   a. Either Stephanie or him is waiting.
   b. Either Stephanie or he is waiting.
   c. Either him or her are waiting.
   d. Either he or Stephanie are waiting.
   e. Either him or Stephanie is waiting.

30. Bridget offered the pecan pie to whoever she wanted.

    a. Bridget offered the pecan pie to whoever she wanted.
    b. Bridget offered the pecan pie to whomever she wanted.
    c. Bridget offered whoever the pecan pie, as she wanted.
    d. Bridget offered everyone the pecan pie, simply because she wanted.
    e. Bridget offered whomever she wanted the pecan pie.

31. Mr. Walker has no objection to him joining the class if he is willing to complete the assignments.

    a. to him joining the class
    b. if he will join the class
    c. for him to join the class
    d. if he were to join the class.
    e. to his joining the class.

32. After the award ceremony, the five scholarship recipients congratulated each other on their good fortune.

    a. the five scholarship recipients congratulated each other on their good fortune.
    b. the five scholarship recipients congratulated each other on account of their good fortune.
    c. the five scholarship winners congratulated each other on enjoying the same good fortune.
    d. the five scholarship winners congratulated one another on their good fortune.
    e. the five scholarship winners, who enjoyed the same good fortune, congratulated one another.

33. Natasha has not and she will not take illegal drugs.

    a. Natasha has not ever and she will not
    b. Natasha has never yet and never will
    c. Natasha never has or will
    d. Natasha has not taken and she will not
    e. Natasha never has and she never will

34. We took a bus to the history museum which carried more than two thousand passengers.

    a. We took a bus to the history museum which carried more than two thousand passengers.
    b. We took a bus to the history museum that carried more than two thousand passengers.
    c. We took a bus to the history museum which held more than two thousand passengers.
    d. We took a bus that carried more than two thousand passengers to the history museum.
    e. We were part of two thousand passengers who took a bus to the history museum.

35. Every flight attendant except Adrienne and she was delayed by bad weather.

    a. except Adrienne and she
    b. except Adrienne and her
    c. accept Adrienne and she
    d. besides she and Adrienne
    e. accept for her and Adrienne

36. If Benjamin Franklin were to walk the halls of a modern university, he would be delighted by the novels uses of electricity, particularly the use of computers.

    a. were to walk the halls of a modern university, he would be delighted by
    b. was to walk the halls of a modern university, he would be delighted by
    c. were to walk the halls in a modern university, he would have to be delighted by
    d. was to walk the halls of a modern university, he would delight to see the
    e. were to walk the halls in a modern university, he would be delighted in

37. The school officials attributed the low GMAT scores to the fact that not one of the more than five hundred students were graduates of the online review class.

   a. The school officials attributed the low GMAT scores to the fact that not one of the more than five hundred students were graduates of the online review class.
   b. The school officials blamed the low GMAT scores to the fact that not one of the more than five hundred students were graduates of the online review class.
   c. The school officials attributed the low GMAT scores to the online review class, which only one of the more than five hundred students were graduates of.
   d. The school officials attributed the low GMAT scores to the fact that not one of the more than five hundred students would have graduated the online review class.
   e. The school officials attributed the low GMAT scores to the fact that not one of the more than five hundred students was a graduate of the online review class.

38. What happens is going to surprise all of you.

   a. What happens is going to surprise all of you.
   b. What happens is going to surprise you.
   c. What will happen is going to surprise all of you.
   d. What happens is going to be a surprise.
   e. What happens is a surprise for all of you.

39. Mia asked Gia to mail her tax return immediately, because she was afraid it would arrive after the deadline.

   a. Mia asked Gia to mail her tax return immediately, because she was afraid it would arrive after the deadline.
   b. Mia asked Gia to mail her tax return immediately, to avoid missing the deadline.
   c. Mia asked Gia to mail her tax return immediately, because she was afraid that Gia would miss the deadline.
   d. Mia advised Gia to mail her tax return immediately, because it would arrive after the deadline.
   e. Mia advised Gia to mail her tax return immediately, to ensure that it arrived before the deadline.

40. If I was her, I would lay my keys on the table before I opened the mail.

   a. If I was her, I would lay
   b. If I was she, I would lay
   c. If I were her, I would lie
   d. If I were she, I would lay
   e. If I were she, I would lie

41. Although Jennifer and Jessica worked together on the science project, Jennifer's conclusions were completely different than Jessica's.

   a. Although Jennifer and Jessica worked together on the science project, Jennifer's conclusions were completely different than Jessica's.
   b. Despite working together on the science project, Jennifer's conclusions were completely different than Jessica's.
   c. Although Jennifer and Jessica worked together on the science project, Jennifer's conclusions were completely different from Jessica's.
   d. Although they worked together on the science project, Jennifer and Jessica reached conclusions that were completely different than each other's.
   e. Jennifer and Jessica, who worked together on the science project, reached conclusions that were completely different than each other.

STOP

The answers to the questions in this section are presented at the end of this publication.

Quantitative Section: 37 questions   75 minutes

Use the following answer choices for questions 1 -12 below:

A. Statement 1 alone is sufficient but Statement 2 alone is not sufficient to answer the question asked.
B. Statement 2 alone is sufficient but Statement 1 alone is not sufficient to answer the question asked.
C. Statements 1 and 2 together are sufficient to answer the question but neither statement is sufficient alone.
D. Each statement alone is sufficient to answer the question.
E. Statements 1 and 2 are not sufficient to answer the question asked and additional data is needed to answer the question.

1. What is the square root of (M + N)?

(1) M - N = 2
(2) M and N are different prime integers between 20 and 24.

2. What is the cost of one hot dog and one soda?

(1) Four hot dogs and three sodas cost $7.00
(2) Twelve hot dogs and twelve sodas cost $15.00.

3. On a snowy Sunday night, Sam, Joe, and Pete decided to compare CD collections. How many CDs does Joe have?

(1) Joe has 10 fewer CDs than Sam
(2) Pete has 12 less than four times the number of CDs that Joe has

4. Five numbers have a sum of 475. What is the middle number?

(1) The numbers are consecutive odd integers
(2) The average of the numbers is 157

5. What is the value of X when Y is 625?

(1) X varies inversely with the square root of Y
(2) X is 5 when Y is 25

6. A cube and a rectangular solid are equal in volume. What is the length of an edge of the cube?

(1) The lengths of the edges of the rectangular solid are 8, 9, and 24
(2) The surface area of the rectangular solid is 960

7. A bartender will mix Liquor A, which is X% alcohol, with Liquor B, which is Y% alcohol, to yield a 1,500 gallon batch of Liquor C, which is Z% alcohol. How many gallons of Liquor B must he use?

(1) X = 5
(2) Y = 20

8. Employees at McDonalds either cook, clean or both. X percent of the employees cook; Y percent of the employees clean. What percentage of employees cooks and cleans?

(1) Half as many employees cook as clean
(2) There are 50 employees at McDonalds

9. A coin with one side heads and the other side tails is tossed A times. What is the probability of getting 4 consecutive tails?

(1) A = 5
(2) 1/32

10. What is the sum of the 500th term through the 505th term in the series?

(1) The first 18 terms are 4, 5, 6, 7, 8, 9, 4, 5, 6, 7, 8, 9, 4, 5, 6, 7, 8, 9
(2) The pattern continues indefinitely

11. How many sides are in polygon J?

(1) The sum of the interior angles is 1,980 degrees
(2) The area of polygon is 1,980

12. In quadrilateral ABCD, what is the value of angle D?

(1) The length of side AB is 12
(2) The sum of angles A, B and C = 2D.

Directions: For each problem, decide which answer is the best of the choices given.

13. If p = 3 and q is 2, what is $(9^p)(27^q)$ =

    a. 3^9
    b. 3^{14}
    c. $(729)^2$
    d. 6561 x 2
    e. 9^5

14. What is the total cost (in cents) of W watermelons, which cost X dollars each, and Y apples, which cost Z cents each?

   a. WXYZ/100
   b. 100WX + YZ
   c. WX + 100YZ
   d. W + YZ/100
   e. 100WX/YZ

15. Reduce the following fraction to its simplest form: 2,000 / 2 million

   a. 1/1000
   b. 2/1000
   c. 1/100
   d. 2/100
   e. 1/10

16. How much greater than 10 − 8y is 5y - 3?

   a. 3y - 11
   b. 13y - 5
   c. 13y - 13
   d. -3y - 11
   e. 13y + 11

17. Over the course of a busy shift, three cashiers at a grocery store gave each other money from their cash drawers to avoid running to the bank. After Cashier 1 gave $15 to Cashier 2 and Cashier 2 gave $12 to Cashier 3, Cashier 1 had $22 more than Cashier 2 and $30 more than Cashier 3. Originally, how much more did Cashier 1 have than Cashier 3?

   a. $25
   b. $27
   c. $33
   d. $43
   e. $47

18. What is the sum of the largest 5 prime numbers that are less than 100?

   a. 393
   b. 419
   c. 421
   d. 443
   e. 449

19. When x is divided by 17, the remainder is 9. What is the remainder when 5x is divided by 17?

   a. 3
   b. 7
   c. 9
   d. 11
   e. 13

20. The denominator of a fraction is three times as large as the numerator. If 5 is added to both the numerator and denominator, the value of the fraction is ¾. What was the numerator of the original fraction?

   a. 1
   b. 2
   c. 3
   d. 4
   e. 5

21. The ratio of W to V is twenty-five times the ratio of V to W. Which of the following terms is equal to V/W?

   a. 1/25
   b. 1/5
   c. 5/1
   d. 25/1
   e. 125

22. At a Van Halen concert with $2,275,000 in total ticket sales, the number of tickets sold in Section A was 100 less than three times the number of tickets sold for Section B, and the number of tickets sold in Section C was half the number of tickets sold in Section B. If Section B tickets cost $300, Section A tickets cost $250 and Section C ticket cost $200, how many tickets were sold in Section C?

   a. 500
   b. 1000
   c. 1500
   d. 2000
   e. 3000

23. Three surgeons – April, May, and June – are asked to perform a heart transplant. Working alone, April could complete the operation in 8 hours. May could do the job in 10 hours if she worked alone, while it would take June 12 hours by herself. On this particular shift, all three of the surgeons worked together on the transplant for two hours. At that point, June left to answer a page and never returned. An hour later, May left to handle another emergency – she also never returned. How long (in minutes) did it take April to complete the heart transplant, after May and June both left?

   a. 56
   b. 60
   c. 66
   d. 70
   e. 76

24. Connie has two investments, A and B. Her income from A, which pays 6%, is $10,000 more than her income from B, which pays 4%. If Connie has $750 more invested in A than B, what is the TOTAL amount of Connie's two investments?

   a. $497,750
   b. $498,500
   c. $996,250
   d. $1,006,250
   e. $1,026,160

25. At a local modeling agency with 500 models, 300 have green eyes and the rest have blue eyes. If 400 of the models are over six feet tall and ten percent of the blue eyed models are less than six feet tall, how many of the green eyed models are over six feet tall?

   a. 20
   b. 80
   c. 100
   d. 180
   e. 220

26. The mean GMAT score for a group of M students in Massachusetts is 1400, while the mean GMAT score for a group of V students in Virginia is 1650. When the scores of both groups are combined, the mean is 1600. What is the value of V/M?

   a. 1/4
   b. 1/2
   c. 1
   d. 2
   e. 4

27. The Q members of the senior class agree to split the cleanup costs equally for their graduation dance, which will be P dollars. If R students fail to graduate and do not pay their share, but the cleanup costs remain the same, how many additional dollars will each of the remaining students have to contribute to pay the cleanup costs?

   a. P/(Q – R)
   b. (P/Q)(R - Q)
   c. PQ/(Q – R)
   d. PR/Q(Q – R)
   e. PQR/Q(Q – R)

28. Vivian and Veronica have a combined age of 50. In ten years, one-half of Vivian's age will be equal to three-quarters of Veronica's current age. How old is Vivian now?

   a. 18
   b. 24
   c. 26
   d. 30
   e. 32

29. A United Airlines jet leaves O'Hare Airport at 6 am and travels directly west at a speed of 700 mph. A US Air jet leaves the same airport at 9 am and travels due north. At 10 am, the two jets are exactly 3,000 miles apart. What is the speed of the USAir jet (in mph)?

   a. 700
   b. 774
   c. 1,077
   d. 1,474
   e. It cannot be determined from the information given.

30. Kelly obtained a recipe for a black velvet wedding cake from the Rachael Ray show. The original recipe made a single round layer cake with a diameter of 8 inches. For her upcoming wedding, Kelly wants to expand the recipe to make a single round layer cake with a diameter of 28 inches. If the original cake required 4 cups of sugar, how many cups of sugar will the larger cake require (assuming the two cakes are equal in thickness)?

   a. 12
   b. 18
   c. 24
   d. 48
   e. 49

31. A kennel owner has 1,400 feet of fencing to create a rectangular dog run. According to the architect's plan, the length of the run is 100 feet more than twice its width. What will the length of the dog run be (in feet)?

   a. 100
   b. 200
   c. 300
   d. 400
   e. 500

32. The length, width, and height of a standard size shipping carton are A, B, and C, respectively. If A, B, and C are all different prime integers between 1 and 15, which of the following could NOT be the volume of the shipping carton?

   a. 105
   b. 110
   c. 120
   d. 130
   e. 190

Refer to the following table for questions 33 – 34.

	2006	2007	2008	2009
Number of shovels sold (thousands)	A	B	C	D
Annual snowfall (inches)	E	F	G	H

33. In 2009, how many thousands of shovels were sold per foot of snow?

   a. D/H
   b. D/12H
   c. 12H/D
   d. DH/12
   e. 12D/H

34. If the number of shovels sold in 2007 was overstated by 25% and the annual snowfall was understated by 50%, what is the correct number of shovels sold per inch of snow that year?

   a. B/2F
   b. F/2B
   c. BF/2
   d. 0.75BF
   e. 0.75B/F

Refer to the following table for questions 35 – 37.

Number of Items Sold (in thousands)

	Macys	Target
Dishes	325	650
Pans	475	425
Towels	750	500

Total Sales (in millions)

	Dishes	Pans	Towels
Macys	8.125	14.250	26.250
Target	13.000	8.500	8.750

35. If Macys and Target both earn 20% profit on all dish sales, what is the total profit (in millions) from dish sales at both stores for the period of time that this table represents (assuming the sale price of dishes at both stores remain the same)?

   a. $1,625,000
   b. $2,600,000
   c. $3,250,000
   d. $4,225,000
   e. $6,500,000

36. Of the three items – Dishes, Pans, and Towels – which commands the highest price per unit at Macys?

   a. Dishes
   b. Pans
   c. Towels
   d. All three items sell for the same price per unit
   e. It cannot be determined from the information given

37. Of the three items – Dishes, Pans, and Towels – which two sell for the same price per unit at Target?

   a. Dishes and Pans
   b. Pans and Towels
   c. Towels and Dishes
   d. All three items sell for the same price per unit
   e. It cannot be determined from the information given

STOP

The answers to the questions in this section
are presented at the end of this publication.

Analysis of an Issue   **30 minutes**

Many people believe that children who are home schooled by their parents will be more productive and happier than children who attend school in a traditional classroom. But others assert that the close supervision and social dynamics of a classroom are necessary to ensure productivity and to develop superior interpersonal skills.

Assignment: Which argument do you find more compelling: the case for home schooling or the opposing viewpoint? Explain your position using relevant reasons or examples from your own experiences, observations, or reading.

Analysis of an Argument   **30 minutes**

Conjugal visits should not be discontinued in prisons that house dangerous felons, including death row inmates. Those convicted of serious crimes should serve their prison sentences, but they should not be denied their right to basic human contact. Most violent criminals are comforted by touch and need to reinforce their positive bonds with their spouses and families. To deny them this basic human right is to deprive prisoners of a harmless outlet for their aggression and make them more dangerous.

Assignment: Explain how logical and persuasive you find this argument. When you present your viewpoint, analyze the argument's line of reasoning and use of evidence. Also, explain what, if anything, would make the argument more convincing or help you to evaluate its conclusion.

Verbal Section Answer Key

Critical Reading

1. Choice C is correct. The other answer choices are not broad enough to convey the overall theme of the passage.

2. Choice B is correct. The answer is presented in the first sentence of the passage.

3. Choice A is correct. The answer is presented in the second paragraph (Lines 18 – 19).

4. Choice C is correct. The answer is presented in the second line of the third paragraph (Lines 22 – 26).

5. Choice C is correct. The answer is presented in the fourth paragraph (Lines 34 –36).

6. Choice B is correct. In this context, *confluxibility* means connectedness.

7. Choice D is correct. The answer is stated directly in the final paragraph (Lines 42 –43).

8. Choice C is correct. The main point of the passage is stated in the final line. If the Italian cities had unified rather than quarreled, they might have maintained their liberty.

9. Choice D is correct. The answer is presented in the first paragraph (Lines 4 –8).

10. Choice E is correct. The answer is presented in paragraph two (Lines 12 – 15).

11. Choice B is correct. All of the other answer choices are mentioned in the first line of paragraph three (Line 21).

12. Choice E is correct. In this context, the word *yokes* means oppression or servitude.

Critical Reasoning

13. For this argument, the best way to strengthen the conclusion is to obtain identical results for several additional Asian women. Choice D is correct.

14. Choice E is correct. The argument generalizes from a very small sample to the entire human population. If the participants who responded are NOT typical of the general population, then the conclusion is weakened. Choice E captures this sentiment.

15. To determine if a statement (or answer choice) is one of the author's assumptions, we must remove the information from the argument and see what happens. Does it fall apart? If so, that statement is one of the author's assumptions. If, on the other hand, the argument is not changed by the omission, then the statement (or answer choice) is not an assumption of the author.

In this question, the argument tells us that the number of uninsured Americans increased between 2001 and 2006. As evidence, the author cites the number of people who lacked medical insurance during those two years. The unstated assumption that the author makes is that the increase in the number of uninsured was *not* due to an increase in population - it was strictly because the original people they polled had lost their insurance between 2001 and 2006. Choice C correctly states this assumption.

16. The argument in the question stem can be symbolized as follows: "All A do B. C is an A. Therefore, C must do B." Of the five possibilities, Choice C is the best answer.

Choice A: All A are B. C are also B. Therefore, C must be A.
Choice B: All A are B. Some A are C. Therefore, this A is a B.
Choice C: All A are B. C is an A. Therefore, C must be B.
Choice D: All A are B. B is a C. Therefore, all A are C.
Choice E: All A are B. C is B. Therefore, C must be an A.

17. To resolve the discrepancy in this argument, we must find the answer choice that allows all of the (seemingly inconsistent) statements to be true. The argument makes sense – and the discrepancy is explained – if patients with lung cancer (but not pancreatic cancer) have an enzymatic abnormality that causes nausea and dizziness when citrus fruit is consumed. Choice C is correct.

18. The original argument is in the following form: "Some A are B. All B are C. Therefore, this A must be C." The correct answer choice must use the same form. Let's evaluate each one:

Choice A: All A have B. Some A are C. Therefore, this C must be B.
Choice B: Some A are B. All B are C. Therefore, this A must be C.
Choice C: Some A have B. All A have C. Therefore, this A must have B.
Choice D: Some A are B. C is an A. Therefore, C must be B.
Choice E: All A are B. Some C are D. Therefore, this A must be C.

Choice B is correct.

19. In this question, we are looking for the answer choice that is one of the author's assumptions. (If we remove this piece of information from the argument, it falls apart.) Choice C is correct. The argument presumes that the article must be written by a *Newsweek* editor in the Tokyo office.

20. Let's begin by dissecting the argument. A = multifaceted; B = majestic; C = fail to please her; D = magenta. Thus, the argument can be written as: "All A and B are C. So, some C are D." The question asks us to determine which answer choice is an assumption in this argument:

Choice A: Some B are D, but not A.
Choice B: Some A and B are D.
Choice C: Some A are D, but not B.
Choice D: All D are C
Choice E: Everything A is D.

Choice B is correct. The argument only makes sense if we assume that some multifaceted and majestic things are magenta.

21. The attorney believes that the review will unfairly influence the jury. If similar juries had already been negatively impacted by an identical study, it would greatly bolster the attorney's argument. Choice C is correct.

22. Choice E is correct. The past frequency of pandemics cannot be used to predict the likelihood of a specific pandemic happening in the future.

23. In this question, the test writers have increased the level of difficulty by using the word "except," which requires you to select the answer that does NOT resolve the discrepancy. Choice D is correct – it is the only choice that does not offer a plausible explanation for the results.

24. Choice A is correct. The physician presumed that one factor *caused* the other, without providing any evidence to support that conclusion.

25. This is the most tedious argument you are likely to see on the GMAT. First, let's dissect it: A = exterminators; B = experienced beekeepers; C = ambidextrous; D = licensed taxidermists

Thus, the original argument can be written as: "Most A who are B are C. But some non-C As are also B. In addition, every B is a D." The question asks us which of the following answer choices must also be true:

Choice A: Some D are C
Choice B: Every D is C
Choice C: Most A are D
Choice D: Every D is an A
Choice E: The B who are D are also C

From the original argument, we can logically state that some D (licensed taxidermists) are C (ambidextrous). Choice A is correct.

26. To determine if a statement (or answer choice) is one of the author's assumptions, remove the information from the argument. Does it fall apart? If so, that statement is one of the author's assumptions. If, on the other hand, the argument is not changed by the omission, then the statement (or answer choice) is not an assumption of the author. In this question, Choice D is correct. The argument presumes that the visitors from the technical conference can only stay at a five-star hotel in San Francisco. The other answer choices are carefully worded distractions.

Sentence Correction

27. The verb tense should be the past perfect tense, which indicates that an action or event was completed before another action or event began. Choice E is correct.

28. Choice E is correct. The original sentence is an overwritten (and somewhat pompous) version of a very simple concept.

29. The full version of the sentence is *Either Stephanie is waiting or he is waiting*. Both subjects require the verb *is*. Hence, the correct answer choice is B.

30. In this sentence, the word *whoever* (which is a subject) is incorrectly used as an object of the preposition *to*. The word *whomever* should be used instead. Answer choice B is correct.

31. In this sentence, we have a pronoun (*him*) modifying a gerund (*joining*). The sentence is incorrect in its original form, because the pronoun should be in the possessive case (*his*, not *him*) to properly modify the noun. *Mr. Walker has no objection to his joining the class.* The correct answer choice is E.

32. Choice D is correct. The original sentence contains an incorrect word choice. *Each other* should be used when referring to two people, while *one another* should be used when referring to more than two people. Choices D and E make this correction, but Choice D does so succinctly.

33. In this sentence, the correct answer must include both forms of the verb *to take*. The only answer choice to do so is D, which is correct. The resulting sentence correctly presents both verb tenses: *Natasha has not taken and she will not take illegal drugs.*

34. The original sentence includes a misplaced modifier, which suggests that the museum carries the passengers, rather than the bus. The sentence should be re-written to place the modifier closer to the word that it modifies: *We took a bus that carried more than two thousand passengers to the history museum.* Choice D is correct.

35. Prepositional phrases require objects, rather than subjects. Hence, the correct pronoun is *her*, not *she*. Answer choice B is correct. Note that the writers also tried to confuse students by using the word *accept* in two of the answer choices.

36. The sentence is correct as originally written. Choice A is correct.

37. The original sentence has an error in subject / verb agreement. The subject (*one*) is singular and requires a singular verb (*was*). Choice E is correct.

38. The correct revision is Choice C, *what will happen*.

39. Choice C is correct. This sentence contains two ambiguous pronouns (*her* and *she*). The correct answer choice must clarify to whom each refers without changing the meaning of the sentence. Of the possibilities, Choice C is the only option that fixes the error without altering the original sentence.

40. The original sentence used the wrong pronoun. Because the first clause is not fact, we must use the subjunctive form of the verb (If *I were*, not If *I was*). Further, the phrase "to be" requires that the pronoun be a subject, not an object (*she*, not *her*). Choice D is correct because it makes this change without introducing an error with the verbs lie and lay.

41. Choice C is correct. The original sentence contains the erroneous expression *different than*, which should be *different from*.

Quantitative Section Answer Key

1. Choice B is correct. Statement 2 gives us enough information to answer the question. (M and N are 21 and 23, respectively, which makes their sum = 44 and the square root = 6.63.)

2. Choice C is correct; we need both statements to solve the problem, which requires us to write one equation for the first condition and a second equation for the second condition.

Although you do not have to calculate the answer for a Data Sufficiency question, we are presenting the solution in case you encounter a comparable problem in multiple choice format. The first step is to define our variables. We will let = x the cost of one hot dog and y = the cost of one soda.

The first equation, which defines the first condition, is $4x + 3y = 7$
The second equation, which defines the second condition, is $12x + 12y = 15$

To solve the problem for x, we must combine the equations in a way that eliminates y. First, we will multiply equation 1 by 4. When we do, our equations become:

16x + 12y = 28
12x + 12y = 25

Next, we will subtract equation 2 from equation 1. When we do, we get 4x = 3. Therefore, x = ¾ = 75 cents = the cost of one hot dog.

To solve for y, the cost of one soda, we must plug the value for x back into one of our equations. When we do, we discover that:

(4)(0.75) + 3y = 7
3 + 3y = 7
3y = 4
y = 4/3 = $1.33 = the cost of one soda
The cost of one hot dog *and* one soda is therefore $0.75 + $1.33 = **$2.08**.

3. To answer this question, we need to know the exact number of CDs that one of the boys owns AND enough information to write an equation to solve for the number that belong to Joe. Neither of these statements gives us an exact number for any of the boys; additionally, there is insufficient information to write an equation to solve for the unknown. Choice E is correct.

4. To answer this question, we need to know the relationship of the five numbers, which Statement 1 provides. Statement 2, however, is NOT enough information for us to find the middle number, because it only gives us an average of the 5 values, not the spread. Choice A is correct.

5. Choice C is correct. Statements 1 and 2 give us enough information to solve the problem. By definition, $X = k/\sqrt{Y}$, so $5 = k/\sqrt{25}$, or $5 = k/5$, or $k = (5)(5) = 25$. Thus, $X = (25)/\sqrt{625} = 25/25 =$ **1**.

6. Each statement, on its own, provides enough information to answer the question. Choice D is correct.

7. At first blush, it seems like we can solve the problem by using Statements 1 and 2, which give us the percentages of alcohol in Liquors A and B. But, we actually need a *third* piece of information to solve the problem, which is the % of alcohol in the final blend, which is Z. Since neither statement provides us with this value, Choice E is correct.

8. To answer this question, we need to know the values of X and Y; we must also know the total number of employees. Statement 2 provides the number of employees, while Statement 1 tells us the *relationship* between X and Y. Unfortunately, it does not give us an exact number for either group. Therefore, we do not have enough information to answer the question. Choice E is correct.

9. In this situation, all we need to know is the number of tosses, which is the value of A. Since Statement 1 provides it, Choice A is correct. Ironically, Statement 2 gives us the actual answer to the question to try to mislead you. (Remember, our goal is not to solve the problem, simply to determine if we have enough information to do so.)

10. To determine the next term in a series or sequence, we need two pieces of information: (1) the pattern that the numbers follow, and (2) whether or not the pattern will continue. Statement 1 gives us the first 18 terms of the series, which follows a definite pattern – the same string of six digits repeat in the same order (456789). Statement 2 provides the second essential piece of information, which is that the series or sequence will continue indefinitely. Therefore, Choice C is correct. With both statements, we can determine the sum of the 500th term through the 505th term, which will simply be the sum of 4+5+6+7+8+9 =**39**.

11. To determine the number of sides in the polygon, we need to know the sum of the interior angles. Statement 1 provides this information. Statement 2 is extraneous information that is designed to confuse you. Choice A is correct.

12. In quadrilateral ABCD, the sum of the interior angles is 360 degrees. Hence, the information in Statement 2 is all we need to determine the value of angle D. Statement 1 provides extraneous information, which we do not need to answer the question. Choice B is correct.

13. If p =3 and q is 2, then $(9^p)(27^q)$ = (9)(9)(9) (27)(27) = 531,441, which is **$(729)^2$**. Choice C is correct.

14. Let's substitute numbers for the variables and see what we get. Let's assume that we have 10 watermelons that cost $3.00 each and 5 apples that cost 60 cents each. Hence, W = 10, X = 3.00, Y = 5 and Z = 0.60.

The total cost of W watermelons is 100(10)(3) = 100WX
The total cost of C apples is (5)(60) = YZ
Therefore, the total cost of the watermelons and apples is 100(10)(3) + (5)(6) = **100WX + YZ**. Choice B is correct.

15. 2,000 / 2,000, 000 = **1/1000**. Choice A is correct.

16. Here, we are simply being asked to find the difference between the two quantities: 5y – 3 - (10 - 8y) = 5y - 3 – 10 + 8y = **13y – 13**. Choice C is correct.

17. To solve this problem, let's assume that Cashier 1 ends her shift with $100. Then, we know that Cashier 2 and Cashier 3 end their shifts with $78 and $70 in their cash drawers, respectively. We can now work backwards to determine how much money each cashier had at the beginning of the shift.

C 1	C 2	C 3	
100	78	70	End of shift; C1 has $22 more than C2 and $30 more than C3
115	63	70	During the shift, C1 gave $15 to C2; let's reverse it
115	75	58	During the shift, C 2 gave C3 $12; let's reverse that
115	75	58	The amount of money each Cashier had at the beginning of the shift

In both cases, we conclude that Cashier 1 initially had $30 more than Cashier 2 and **$47** more than Cashier 3. Choice E is correct.

18. To solve, we must simply count back from 100 and add together the 5 largest prime numbers:

90 – 100: prime numbers include 97
80 – 90: prime numbers include 89, 83
70 - 80: prime numbers include 79 and 73

The largest prime numbers less than 100 are therefore 97 + 89 + 83 + 79 + 73 = **421**. Choice C is correct.

19. To solve this problem, simply choose a number that meets the original condition: it leaves a remainder of 9 when it is divided by 17. In this case, the number **26** meets the condition. Next, let's submit the number 26 to the second condition and see what happens. (26)(5)/17 = 130.

130 = (17)(7) + 11. 130 leaves a remainder of 11 when it is divided by 17. Choice D is correct.

20. This problem is easy to solve if you stay calm, read carefully, and set up your equation correctly. First, let x be the original numerator. The original fraction is therefore x/3x. The new fraction is (x + 5)/(3x + 5), which equals ¾. We must solve the equation for x. When we cross-multiply, we get: 4x + 20 = 9x + 15, or x = 1. Choice A is correct.

21. W/V = 25V/W
W = $25V^2$/W
W^2 = $25V^2$
1/25 = V^2/W^2
1/5 = V/W. Choice B is correct.

22. Although the verbiage in this question is confusing, it is actually just a simple problem in which concert tickets were sold at three different prices. Knowing the total sales, we must determine how many were sold at one of the three price points. To solve, we must first define our variables.

For simplicity, we will let X = the number of tickets sold in Section B. Their value is 300x.
Therefore, the number of tickets in Section A = 3x – 100. Their value is 250(3x – 100).
Finally, the number of tickets in Section C = 1/2x. Their value is 200(1/2x) or 100x.

Our equation is simply:

Section A + Section B + Section C = Total Sales
250(3x – 100) + 300x + 100x = $2,275,000
750x - 25,000 + 400x = $2,275,000
1150x = $2,300,000
x = 2000 tickets sold in Section B. The number of tickets sold in Section C = 2000/2 = **1000**. Choice B is correct.

23. This work problem is as tedious and time-consuming as you are likely to see on a standardized test. Nevertheless, it is relatively easy to solve if you keep track of what you are calculating in each step.

First, we must calculate how much of the surgery was completed during the first two hours, when April, May and June were working together.

If April can do the operation alone in 8 hours, then she did 2(1/8) = 2/8 = ¼ of the work in the first two hours.

If May can do the operation alone in 10 hours, then she did 2(1/10) = 2/10 = 1/5 of the job during the first two hours.

Finally, if June can do the operation alone in 12 hours, then she did 2(1/12) = 2/12 = 1/6 of the job during the first two hours.

The total of those three fractions is the amount of the surgery that was done in the first two hours: ¼ + 1/5 + 1/6 = 15/60 + 12/60 + 10/60 = 37/60.

Next, we must determine how much of the job that April and May completed during the third hour, when they worked together. That amount is 1/8 + 1/10 = 5/40 + 4/40 = 9/40.

Thus, by the time April was alone in the operating room, the amount of work completed was 37/60 + 9/40 = 74/120 + 27/120 = 101/120. To determine how much time April will need to finish the job, we must subtract that number from 1, which is: 120/120 – 101/120 = 19/120.

By definition, based on April's individual rate (8 hours to complete the job alone), 19/120 = x/8. If we solve this equation for x, we find that it will take April 19/15, or **76**/60 hours to complete the heart transplant, which is 1 hour and 16 minutes.   Choice E is correct.

24. First, we must draw a table with the information that we know.

Investment	Amount	Interest Rate	Total Return
A	x + $750	6	6(x + 750)
B	x	4	4x

Here, we are asked to determine the total amount of money invested in A + B. First, we will solve for B. We will therefore let x = the amount of money invested in B, which means that the amount of money invested in A = x + 750.

From the problem, we know that Connie's income from A is $10,000 more than her income from B. Therefore, our equation is:

Income from A – Income from B = 10,000
0.06(x + 750) – 0.04x = 10,000
0.06x + 45 – 0.04x = 10,000
0.02x = 9955
x = $497,750 = amount of investment B
x + 750 = $498,500 = amount of investment A
A + B = $497,750 +$ 498,500 = **$996,250**. Choice C is correct.

To check our answer, we can simply plug in the amount of interest that each investment earns to see if it matches the stipulations in the question stem.
The total return for A is 0.06($498,500) = $29,910.
The total return for B is 0.04($497,750) = $19,910.
Connie's income from A is indeed $10,000 more than her income from B.

25. The best way to attack this type of problem is to summarize our data in a simple table. In this case, the models have either green eyes or blue eyes. Some are over 6 feet tall, while others are less than 6 feet tall. When we put the information into our chart, we get:

	Green Eyes	Blue Eyes	Total
Under 6 ft.	80	20	100
Over 6 ft.	220	180	400
Total	300	200	500

From the table, we can answer the question; the number of green eyed models over six feet tall is **220**. Choice E is correct.

26. From the data in the problem, we can write an equation to identify the value of V/M:
{1400M + 1650V} / (M + V) = 1600
1400M + 1650V = 1600M + 1600V
50V = 200M
V = 4M
V/M = **4**. Choice E is correct.

27. In this case, the easiest way to solve the problem is to substitute numbers for the variables. For the sake of simplicity, let's assume that Q = 100, P = 1000, and R = 20. Thus, the cost per person is P/ Q = 1000/100 = 10 dollars. If R = 20 students do not pay their share, then the additional cost for the 100 – 20 = 80 remaining students is (20 X 10) = 200. 200/80 = $2.5 dollars.

Now, we can solve the problem by converting this relationship from numbers to letters. The cost per student is P/Q = 10 dollars. If R = 20 students do not pay their share, then the additional cost for the (Q - R) = 80 remaining students is: (P/Q) (R) / (Q – R) = 20 (1000/100) / (100 – 20) = 20 (10) / 80 = $2.50, which is Choice D.

28. In this case, we can write one equation for the first condition and a second equation for the second condition. As always, we must first define our variables. We will let x = Vivian's age and y = Veronica's age.

The first equation, which defines the first condition, is x + y = 50
The second equation, which defines the second condition, is (x + 10)/2 = ¾y

To solve the problem for x, we must combine the equations in a way that eliminates y. The fastest way to accomplish this is to re-write equation 1 as y = 50 – x and substitute this value for y in equation 2. But first, let's multiply equation 2 by 4 to eliminate the fractions. When we do, we get:

2(x + 10) = 3y
Now, let's substitute 50 – x for y:
2x + 20 = 3(50 – x)
2x + 20 = 150 – 3x
5x = 130
x = **26** = Vivian's age. Choice C is correct.
y = 50 – 26 = 24 = Veronica's age.

To check our results, let's confirm that the conditions hold: In 10 years, Vivian will be 36 and Veronica will be 34. Half of Vivian's age (18) is indeed ¾ of Veronica's current age.

29. The scenario can be depicted as a right triangle in which the hypotenuse = 3,000 miles. The United Airlines jet flew west for 4 hours. Since Distance = Rate x Time, Distance = 700 x 4 = 2,800 miles.

In contrast, the jet that flew north traveled for one hour, so its Distance = Rate x Time = Rate X 1, or Distance = Rate. To find this distance, which is the same as the rate, we must solve the following equation:

Distance (United Flight) + Distance (USAir Flight) = Total Distance
$2,800^2 + d^2 = 3,000^2$
$d^2 = 3,000^2 - 2,800^2 = 9,000,000 – 7,8400,000 = 1,160,000$
D = **1077** mph. Choice C is correct.

30. The original cake had a diameter of 8 inches. Hence, its area was (4)(4)π = 16π.
The second cake has a diameter of 28 inches. Hence, its area was (14)(14)π = 196π.
196/16 = 12.25. Kelly will need to multiply the recipe by 12.25 to make the larger cake. (12.25)(4) = **49** cups. Choice E is correct.

31. Using the information we have been given about the perimeter and area of the dog run, we can write two separate formulas for its length and width. Then, we can combine the two equations to solve for each.
Perimeter = 2L + 2W
1,400 = 2(100 + 2W) + 2W
1,400 = 200 + 4W + 2W
6W = 1,200
W = 200

Now, we can plug this value into the original equation to solve for the length:
2(L) + 2(200) = 1,400
2L = 1000
Length = **500**. Choice E is correct.

32. To solve this problem, we must factor each answer choice to see which ones meet the criterion (3 different prime integers between 1 and 15). When we do, we discover that only Choice C could *not* be the volume of the carton.

105 = 3 x 5 x 7
110 = 2 x 5 x 11
120 = 2 x 2 X 2 x 15. Choice C is correct.
130 = 2 x 5 x 13
190 = 2 x 5 x 19

33. In 2009, D shovels were sold per H inches of snow. The number sold per foot of snow = D/(H/12) =**12D/H**. Choice E is correct.

34. The number of shovels sold per inch of snow in 2007 was B/F. If B was overstated by 25% and F was understated by 50%, then the corrected number of shovels sold per inch of snow would be 0.75B/1.5F = B/2F. Choice A is correct.

Alternatively, we can plug substitute numbers for the letters and see what we get. Let's let B = 100 and F = 10. Therefore, a 25% reduction in B = 75 and a 50% increase in F = 15. The corrected ratio is 75/15 = 5. Converting back to letters, 5 = 100/(2)(10), which is **B/2F**.

35. The profit from dish sales at Macys is ($8,125,000 sales)(0.20) = $1,625,000
The profit from dish sales at Target is ($13,000,000 sales)(0.20) = $2,600,000
The total profit is therefore $1,625,000 + $2,600,000 = **$4,225,000**. Choice D is correct.

36. The item with the highest price per unit at Macys are Towels, which are **$35** each ($26,250,000/750,000). Choice C is correct.

37. At Target, Dishes and Pans both sell for **$20**. Choice A is correct.
Dishes: ($13,000,000/650,000 sold) = $20 per unit; Pans: ($8,500,000/425,000 sold) = $20 per unit.

Analysis of an Issue

The Outline:

Position: attending school is better

Introduction: President's Clinton's quote: Education is more than what we learn in books
Home schooling benefits (customization, no peer pressure, self-paced learning) do not outweigh disadvantages

Benefits of school:

1. Breadth of classes / explore & discover new talents

2. Teachers are experts in specific areas: can handle off-beat and intricate questions

3. Unbiased evaluation of performance

4. Social skills and outside groups provide source for maturity and development. Learn how to interact w/ different types of people. Excellent preparation for college and beyond

Conclusion: Recent stats about job change. Need flexibility. People skills. Ability to work on high performance teams. We get this from school

The Essay (received two scores of 6)

During his commencement address at Harvard University, former President Bill Clinton noted that education was far more than what students learn from books; it is the accumulation of every academic, personal, cultural and recreational experience that we bring into our lives. Each interaction and activity that we choose has the power to open our minds to new ideas and perspectives, which eventually broaden our world. From my own experiences at a large metropolitan high school, and those of other students in different learning environments, I am convinced that the optimal place for education is in the classroom, rather than my own home.

Over time, I have considered the merits of several arguments in favor of home schooling. For non-traditional students, particularly those with learning disabilities, it provides an ambient learning environment that is free of social expectations and peer pressure. Home schooling enthusiasts also cite the benefits of self-paced learning, in which the parent and child can create a lesson plan that suits the student's individual needs. But, for me, the drawbacks of a home-based education far outweigh its advantages.

Attending a traditional high school offers numerous academic, social and recreational benefits that few parents can give their children. At Davis High School, I built a challenging curriculum that included 10 Advanced Placement courses in 5 academic areas. My teachers were all national experts in their fields, who were well prepared to answer unusual and intricate questions. They could also provide an objective assessment of my performance, compared to the thousands of other students they had taught in their distinguished careers.

Although my parents are well educated, their mastery of quantitative subjects like math and science does not compare to that of my teachers, Dr. Bennett and Mr. Gray. As an aspiring engineer, I was honored to reap the benefits of such an impressive level of instruction in the classroom and the lab. Without the generosity and support of Davis's faculty, I would not have had the confidence to pursue such a rigorous major.

Davis High School also offered the opportunity to explore my talents in art, music, athletics and debate. In a home-schooling environment, I would have shied away from these challenges, which were originally quite intimidating. By flexing my wings in the company of my fellow students, I not only uncovered a few unexpected talents, but made several close friends in the process. In fact, these connections with my teachers and fellow students were probably the greatest blessing that I reaped from attending school. By working with other students on class projects, team sports, and numerous charitable endeavors, I learned that success is rarely a solitary event; great things happen when a group of people combines their energy in support of a common goal.

In 2004, Jack Welch, the retired CEO of GE, noted that most college graduates will change jobs 8 times in their careers. Accordingly, their greatest assets are flexibility and interpersonal skills, which enable them to quickly adapt to new people, places and situations. I could not learn these skills sitting at the kitchen table listening to a history lecture from my mother. I could only achieve my personal best by going to school, engaging with others, and sampling the world of opportunities that were available to me, if I was only willing to ask.

Why is this essay so good? The author relates every paragraph back to his position that traditional schooling is best. Citing his many achievements at Davis High School, he makes a compelling argument that he would not have received as broad and satisfying an education at home. Amazingly, the author also acknowledged the alternative viewpoint in a respectful and intelligent manner. His level of insight, particularly regarding Jack Welch's comments on career strengths, is highly unusual for a college senior.

Analysis of an Argument

The Outline:

1. I **disagree** with the author's conclusion that convicted felons deserve the right to conjugal visits.

2. **His arguments**:

a) all humans need touch,, which makes them less aggressive
b) to deprive them of touch would make them more dangerous
c) prisoners retain these rights while they are incarcerated

3. **My concerns**:

a) prisoners forfeit their rights upon conviction
b) there is no proof that conjugal visits make prisoners less aggressive
c) the high recidivism rate suggests that these programs do not work

4. **Additional evidence** that is needed:

a) that positive relationships reduce violent crime
b) that death row inmates deserve any sort of rights

The Analysis (received two scores of 6)

The author concludes that violent prisoners should be allowed to have conjugal visits to satisfy their needs for basic human contact. His argument is that all people, including violent felons, are comforted by touch and will be less aggressive if they can satisfy their sexual needs. Furthermore, the author suggests that these benefits should extend to death row inmates, although they have no hope for rehabilitation or release.

I detect two unwarranted assumptions in the author's reasoning. First, he assumes that convicted criminals retain their right to intimate contact while they are incarcerated. I vehemently disagree. Criminals forfeit this civil liberty when they are sentenced to prison, along with their right to move freely in society. From a social and physical perspective, an inmate's separation from his friends, family, and loved ones is an integral part of his punishment. To restore it arbitrarily would defeat the entire purpose of his prison sentence.

The author also presumes that providing an inmate with a "harmless outlet" for the release of aggression will make him less violent. Sadly, anecdotal evidence does not support this assumption. With a recidivism rate of almost 60%, our prisons are filled with repeat offenders who could not succeed in society after their release. Their initial prison sentences, which included conjugal visits, left them as angry and violent as they were before.

The author could strengthen his argument by providing quantitative evidence that people who form positive intimate relationships are less likely to commit violent crimes. Alternatively, he could provide statistical evidence to prove that inmates who enjoy conjugal visits are more likely to be successfully rehabilitated than those who do not. Finally, he must offer a valid argument to support his contention that death row inmates, who are the most violent and dangerous criminals of all, deserve this sort of benefit. Without this evidence, the author's conclusion is difficult to support.

This essay, although short, is well-written and conceived. The first paragraphs outline the argument effectively and note the inconsistency between the conclusion and the evidence; the final paragraph offers compelling suggestions to improve the argument. From a mechanical perspective, the organization, sentence structure, and grammar are excellent (Score = 6).

www.ingramcontent.com/pod-product-compliance
Lightning Source LLC
Chambersburg PA
CBHW081351040426
42450CB00015B/3396